KITTY KITTY KITTY

KITTY KITTY KITTY

D1413123

KITTY KITTY KITTY

KITTY KITTY KITTY

KITTY KITTY KITTY

You Know You're a
Cat Lover
When...

Ben Fraser

Illustrations by Roger Penwill

summersdale

YOU KNOW YOU'RE A CAT LOVER WHEN...

Summersdale Publishers Ltd
46 West Street
Chichester
West Sussex
PO19 1RP
UK

www.summersdale.com

Printed and bound in the Czech Republic

ISBN: 978-1-84953-091-0

Substantial discounts on bulk quantities of Summersdale books are available to corporations, professional associations and other organisations. For details contact Summersdale Publishers by telephone: +44 (0) 1243 771107, fax: +44 (0) 1243 786300 or email: nicky@summersdale.com.

To..

From..

You have your hair highlighted
a nice shade of tabby.

You greet all of your friends by saying,
'What's new, pussycat?'

Your son's middle name is 'Simba' in tribute to *The Lion King.*

You are on first-name terms with all the local firemen... because they're always helping you down from trees after you get stuck rescuing your cat.

You spend hours in front of the mirror trying to perfect the art of 'grinning like a Cheshire cat'.

Your ringtone is the *Top Cat* theme tune.

You try to encourage your husband to grow outlandish, feline-inspired facial hair. You do love a man with whiskers.

The first question you ask if you meet
someone new is, 'Would you say you're
a Persian blue or a Brazilian
shorthair person?'

You fit kitty's collar with a GPS tag, so you can find out exactly where it goes at night.

You develop a repetitive strain injury from stroking your cat so enthusiastically.

You take regular cruise holidays with your favourite feline so you can fill your 'Purr-fect Memories' photo album with snaps of the two of you around the world.

Your entire house is kitty themed...
right down to the human-sized cat
basket that you sleep in.

You've told so many variations of *Puss in Boots* that your kids now ask to tuck themselves in at bedtime.

You think Andrew Lloyd Webber should have his own statue on Broadway – putting *Cats* on the stage was a stroke of genius!

You insist on personally taste-testing any new cat food you buy.

You sit on the floor to watch TV whilst
your feline friends lounge on the sofa...
It wouldn't be right to disturb them.

You always share your sweets with kitty – usually a Kit Kat or a bag of white mice.

Your last partner moved out after
discovering that you purr continuously
in your sleep.

You care more about who your cat's socialising with than who your kids are hanging out with.

You have a variety of life-sized
cardboard cut-outs of your favourite
celebrity: Felix from the cat
food advert.

The police turn up to investigate reports of strange-looking plants in your greenhouse... only to discover it's your personal catnip farm.

You have a walk-in wardrobe
full of designer clothes and
bling accessories for your cat.

You have your cat as ring-bearer at your wedding... and a 'best cat'.

Your will states that all your money
will be left to the care of your cat,
who, in the event of your demise, must
be petted on the hour, every hour.

You look forward to your furry alarm clock waking you up at 5.30 a.m. for food every morning.

Instead of getting a manicure, you simply join your cat at the scratching post.

Your partner raises the subject of getting a dog, and you decide it's the end of the road for the relationship.

You decide to buy a stake in a fish farm in Scotland to cater for your pussy's insatiable appetite for fresh organic salmon.

You spend hours re-knitting a jumper
that your cat helpfully undid for you...
It was just trying to help.

You seem so at home in the cat aisle of Pets at Home, that customers keep coming up and asking you for assistance.

You insist an all-day cat crèche be introduced at your workplace... it's just too painful to be apart from your kitty *all* day.

You sign up for annual membership to the Kitty Kat Club on impulse – only to discover it's not the sort of place that welcomes pets... or clothes, for that matter.

Your cat's deluxe litter tray covers over half of the floor space in your kitchen.

You organise an awards ceremony for your kitty's mouse-catching abilities.

Your air freshener of choice is
'Summer Catnip'.

You throw out your family heirlooms to make room in your glass cabinet for your cat's old playthings.

You buy everyone cat-themed gifts for Christmas, including framed photos of your moggy – why wouldn't they want to admire your beautiful pet?

You enter a period of
mourning when one of the
Blue Peter cats dies.

People start to roll their eyes every time you begin a story with, 'This one time my cat...'

You have an ornate stone memorial built in your garden and a 'mewseum' dedicated to your beloved childhood cat, Tiddles.

You write to the makers of *Tom and Jerry* and demand that they create an entire series in which Tom comes out on top in every episode.

You can happily spend an evening discussing the extensive range of cat flaps available on the market.

You'd much rather spend Sunday mornings baking tuna cookies for your cat than cooking Sunday lunch for the family.

Your cupboards are so full of cat food that you've been known to eat Kitty Bites for breakfast, without even batting an eyelid.

You take a course to learn to 'speak cat'.

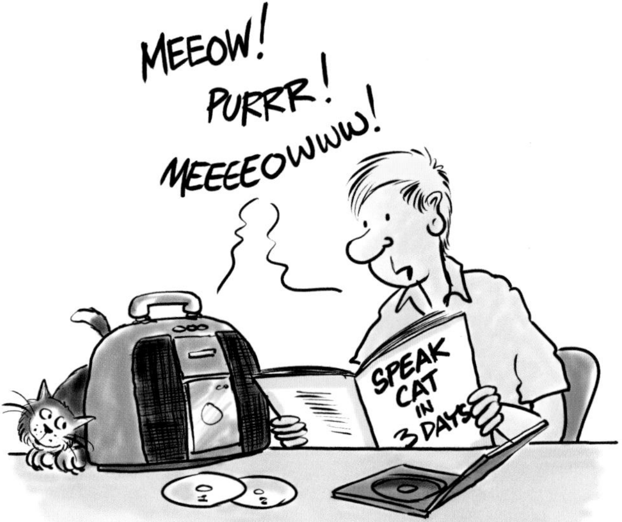

MEEOW!
PURRR!
MEEEEOWWW!
SPEAK CAT IN 3 DAYS

There's only one kind of shoe
in your wardrobe: kitten heels,
naturally.

You buy furniture and home accessories to complement your cat's markings.

You answer the phone with a meow – apparently the hours you spend conversing with your cat are finally rubbing off.

You move on from sushi to eating raw goldfish, but only if the man at the fairground stall isn't looking.

You install a cat basket on the front of your bike so you can take your kitty to choose the 'dine in for two' meal that you're going to share later.

You edit your back catalogue of *Animal Rescue* tapes to make one twelve-hour collection of back-to-back cat stories.

Your cat knocks over your antique glass vase and you just smile and say 'accidents happen'. If it had been your partner on the other hand...

You don't mind if your cat gets to work on your new furniture with its claws after all, the 'distressed' look is very in right now.

You refuse to believe there's such a thing
as a 'cat allergy' – although your mum
goes into a sneezing fit every time
she visits...

You simply can't understand why ITV has refused your pitch for a new show, *My Cat Does the Cutest Things.*

You consider the moniker 'that crazy cat person' to be a highly honourable title.

You can't resist testing the theory that, like Garfield, your cat's favourite food is lasagne.

You always jump up to greet your kitty as soon as you hear the cat flap as it comes in from a hard night's mouse catching.

Your favourite line in Shakespeare is:
'Tabby, or not tabby... that is
the question!'

You try to convince your boss
that 'catnaps' are the new
'power naps'.

You don't mind that your new cashmere jumper becomes your kitty's favourite blanket... well, it is very soft.

You spoil every game of Mouse Trap by getting over-excited and setting off the trap as soon as it's built.

You have no qualms about wearing your kitty paw slippers while out on the town.

You invite your friends and neighbours to be on the panel for your home-made spin-off show, *Strictly Cat Dancing*.

You miss a family reunion because your cat looks a bit 'down', so you both stay in and sing along to your *Mamma Meow* DVD instead.

You count bouncing kittens instead of sheep to help you drop off at night.

You get a tiger-print paint job for your car and pay your local pet store to pimp the insides out, kitty style.

The first thing you do in the morning is shake the cats out of your bed.

Your favourite mode of transport is a Jaguar... a big, black, furry one.

You think that your new cat pyjamas
are, without a doubt, 'the
cat's pyjamas'.

You don't ask questions. Well, curiosity killed the cat.

You dress as Catwoman every year on Halloween and go out on the hunt for anyone dressed as Batman – meowww.

Have you enjoyed this book?
If so, why not write a review
on your favourite website?

Thanks very much for buying
this Summersdale book.

www.summersdale.com